RESEMBLANCES

RESEMBLA

NCES

AMAZING FACES
BY CHARLES LE BRUN
INTRODUCTION BY
EDWARD SOREL

Another Harlin Quist Book

A Harlin Quist Book
Distributed by Dial/Delacorte Sales
One Dag Hammarskjold Plaza
New York, New York 10017.
Copyright © 1980 by Harlin Quist.
Introduction copyright © 1980 by Edward Sorel.
All rights reserved.
No part of this book may be reproduced
or transmitted in any form or by any means,
electronic or mechanical,
including photocopying, recording
or by any information storage
and retrieval system, without
the written permission of the Publisher,
except where permitted by law.
Manufactured in the United States of America.
First printing.

Library of Congress Cataloging in Publication Data

Le Brun, Charles, 1619-1690.
　Resemblances, amazing faces.

　1. Physiognomy—Early works to 1850.　I. Sorel,
Edward, 1929-　　II. Title.
BF840.L4　1980　　138　　80-18698
ISBN 0-8252-7360-9

INTRODUCTION

Charles Le Brun was a Frenchman who achieved prominence as an artist during the reign of Louis XIV; but it is his curious physiognomy studies and the "scientific" theories he evolved from them that are far more interesting to modern audiences than the vast allegorical paintings he contributed to Versailles, the Louvre, and other collections. The physiognomy studies illustrated a dissertation delivered by Le Brun before the Academy of Painters and Sculptors (of which he was a founding member), but unfortunately the notes that originally accompanied the drawings disappeared centuries ago. Scholars have pieced together—from the drawings and from other writings—the theories that Le Brun had worked out, and it is from their work that we are able to draw further conclusions.

Le Brun's physiognomy studies are an offshoot of man's continuing fascination with the congruities that can be found between human and animal "faces" and our seemingly

Plate 1

irresistible desire to equate physical features with personality.

After all, don't many of us really believe that we can tell a person's character by just looking at him or her? Don't we all on some subconscious level allow ourselves to judge how bright someone is by the way he or she appears to us? Mankind, it would seem, has some atavistic need to believe that physiognomy determines personality. The ancient Greeks were certain there was a correlation between the two, and the number of porcelain phrenological busts that one still finds in antique shops attests to the Victorians' belief that one could determine character by feeling the bumps on a person's head. And it didn't end there.

After the science of phrenology was discredited, a German, Ernst Kretschmer, director of the Neurological Institute at the University of Marburg, stepped forward with his theory that a person's temperament was a reflection of his physical makeup. He promulgated this thesis in the 1920s and lived to see the Nazis endorse and then distort it in order to legitimize their own racial theories.

Finally we come to William Sheldon, an American, who published *Varieties of Temperament* in 1941. Reprinted in 1976, the book divided man into three categories: endomorph, mesomorph, and ectomorph. It proposed that a person's physique determines his type, which in turn determines personality tendencies. Sheldon's theory was genuinely scientific in approach and is still respected in academic circles. But Le Brun's notion has an innocent charm one may enjoy even while cognizant of its scientific absurdities.

Charles Le Brun was born in 1619, the son of a Picardy artisan sculptor. The father recognized that young Charles, of his many children, had real talent. With parental maneuvering worthy of Leopold Mozart or a twentieth-century stage mother, Le Brun *père* managed to apprentice Charles to a now forgotten painter named Vouet.

Whether it was additional parental pushing or the young man's own eye for the opportune chance that led him to paint an allegorical interpretation of the glory of Richelieu and boldly deliver it in person to the Cardinal, we do not know, but it led to an invitation to join the

Plate 2

peintres du roi, the monarch's personal artists. Charles won an annual salary, room and board at the Louvre or the Tuileries, and a commission to paint for Richelieu, among other works, the impassioned if rather ghoulish *Hercules Forcing the Horses of Diomedes to Devour Their Master*.

I first encountered Le Brun's work while taking the tour of Versailles that is obligatory for newcomers to Paris. Le Brun had gone on to become *premier peintre du roi*, artist laureate, to Louis XIV. In that capacity he had painted ceiling or wall murals in four enormous rooms at Versailles, and had acted as a kind of super interior decorator for the entire vast project: planning, designing, and overseeing the production of all that he had not actually produced.

It was Le Brun, the tour guide explained, who had executed the vast decorative sequences on the ceilings of the Salon de la Guerre and the Salon de la Paix and on the walls of the Grande Galerie. Impressive as these undertakings undoubtedly were, they were not the sort of thing I much admired. Like the movies of Cecil B. De Mille, I found Le Brun's work long on spectacle but short on substance. I was relieved when the guide informed us that we would be unable to view Le Brun's extraordinary murals of the Escalier des Ambassadeurs, which had—unfortunately, he said—been destroyed by fire.

When I look back now, no particular detail or image comes to mind; at Versailles, of course, the particular is of little consequence—the effect is all. Of his works at the Louvre, among which are four canvases on the life of Alexander (three of them over forty feet long), I remember nothing. There is a lot of competition in the Louvre.

As it turns out, Le Brun was considerably more than a super interior decorator. He was a painter of some sensibility and enormous output, the designer of what were unquestionably the best tapestries in the Europe of his day, and an artistic administrator *par excellence.* He was also enormously prolific; before Versailles he had decorated numerous town houses—he painted his way from the Hôtel Nouveau to the Hôtel Rivière to the Hôtel La Basinère to the

Plate 3

Hôtel D'Aumont to the Hôtel Lambert and finally arrived at the Château de Vaux-le-Vicomte, the country residence of the extremely wealthy minister of finance, M. Fouquet.

Le Brun realized that here was a man worth pleasing. He glorified the minister in paintings throughout his private apartments and designed similarly flattering tapestries for other rooms. When the castle was complete, Le Brun planned and produced a lavish tableau and fireworks for Fouquet's elaborate housewarming. The king was impressed.

But Fouquet's career was doomed, and on the day of its eclipse, Le Brun presented the wife of the new first minister, Jean Baptiste Colbert, with one of his drawings. It was then that Le Brun was made *premier peintre du roi,* and put in charge of all the artistic endeavors Colbert planned to exalt the monarchy, including the Gobelins. This was a rundown factory where the furniture, tapestries, silver plates, and other necessities for the various royal residences were produced. Le Brun revived it and made it one of the country's major and most profitable industries. The Gobelins tapestries, in particular, became famous—the best were designed by Le Brun and produced under his close direction.

One might have thought that Le Brun's endeavors at the Gobelins, the general supervision of all the *peintres du roi*, and his own painting would have been more than enough. But in court circles one must never appear to be settled or one soon finds oneself unsettled by another. So when Colbert wanted his own Château de Sceaux redecorated and gardens complete with fountains installed, there was Le Brun, plans all ready. When the king required costumes and scenery for his pageants, Le Brun always had just the thing in mind. The gigantic tapestry *Alexander Entering Babylon,* now in the Louvre, served as a backdrop for one such entertainment. And when the Louvre itself was being enlarged, it was he who painted the wonderful *Neptune and Amphitrite, Evening and Night in the Gallery of Apollo.*

But another facet of Le Brun's experience at the Château de Vaux eventually led, I would like to suggest, to the remarkable studies in physiognomy that are collected in this book. M. Fouquet, before he fell into disgrace and was arrested and never heard from again, patron-

Plate 4

ized young men of literary as well as artistic promise. Foremost among these was a young writer of Le Brun's own age, a certain Jean de La Fontaine. La Fontaine was often at Vaux during the period Le Brun was working there. He greatly admired the painter's work—that we know from his praises in *Le Songe de Vaux,* a medley of prose and poetry that he began at this time, and from *Élégie aux nymphes de Vaux,* a complaint on the disgrace of their mutual patron that he wrote ten years later.

I would conjecture that Le Brun and La Fontaine, the latter an easy-going, garrulous, and most charming man, probably spent much time in conversation, perhaps while Le Brun was painting. What if La Fontaine, his head churning with ideas of beasts who behaved like men, poured out his thoughts to his friend the artist, or read to him from bits that he had already begun to put down on paper? And what if Le Brun, intrigued, began to sketch those similarities as they appeared to him visually?

Of course, La Fontaine's verbal descriptions of anthropomorphism were one thing and their visual counterpart something else entirely. The latter required an extensive study of facial characteristics and some conclusions as to what sort of face was suggested by the animal. In his "System of Physiognomy" Le Brun methodically divided man into three basic types distinguishable by the position and formation of their eyes. He illustrated this hypothesis by sketching three faces, in which the only significant variation was the eyes *(Plate 1)*. In the center, appropriately, was the man of reason, the man whose passions, both good and bad, were always under control (not *suppressed*, of course, this being long before Freud): a calm, serene, rational man. Type one was level-headed in every sense of the word. A horizontal line drawn across his face at eye level extended from the upper ears and exactly bisected his eyes, passing directly through the inner and outer corners.

Type two *(depicted in Plate 1 on the right)* was a man of noble passions, a man ruled less by reason than by generous impulse or creative force. Men of genius fell into this category (genius being considered a necessarily exemplary attribute, this being long before Nietzsche).

Type two could be discerned by the upward cast of his eyes, in search, Le Brun supposed, if not for God, at least for fame and immortality. A horizontal line bisecting the eyes at the outer corners would fall slightly below the inner corners, while straight lines from the outer to the inner corners of each eye would form an apex somewhere above the horizontal line.

Type three *(the figure on the left in Plate 1)* was the opposite of type two: he was a man governed by ignoble passions, ruled by animal desires (always conceived to be negative, this being long before Rousseau). He could be recognized by the slant of his eyes, which was opposite to that of type two—a horizontal line extending from the same point in the upper ears (Le Brun had some difficulty with ears, the left never quite matching the right) would pass just above the inner corners of the eyes and decidedly below the outer corners. The triangle formed by the two lines drawn through both corners of each eye would have its apex well below its horizontal base. Type three appeared always to cast his eyes downward— perhaps in shame, or perhaps because light itself was foreign to his dark nature.

Of course, all men, Le Brun said, were composites of the three types, but tended toward one or another. As classic examples of his first and third types he chose the easily recognizable Roman emperors Antoninus and Nero. They were, he said, Virtue and Vice personified, perfect examples of the man of reason and the man of ignominy. The mild Antoninus, often known as Antoninus Pius, is contrasted with the degenerate Nero. Antoninus had, of course, not only the proper eyes of the just ruler and man of reason, he also had all the other facial characteristics associated with the classic gods of Greek art—curly locks, high forehead, aquiline nose, short upper lip, double chin, and practically no eyelids at all.

From the Roman emperors Le Brun moves to his first comparison of man and animal; he portrays the classic Greek rendering of the heads of Jupiter and Hercules *(Plates 2 and 3)* and compares them to the lion *(Plate 4)*. Jupiter *(Plate 2)* is a characteristic type one; Hercules *(Plate 3)* has type three eyes, of which the lion *(Plate 4)* is the extreme example. Jupiter, Hercules, and lion all have luxuriant manes.

Plate 5

Next Le Brun considers the animals themselves. Certain deductions could, he said, be made from the mathematical construction of their physiognomy. His theories are often complex and too far-fetched to go into in detail, but perhaps the most interesting is his mathematical proof of whether or not an animal is carnivorous by superimposing equilateral triangles onto its profile *(Plate 4)*. Base line AB runs from the tip of the lion's nostril, point A, to the opening of the ear, point B, passing through the inner corner of the eye at point E. The vertex of the triangle, point C, falls somewhere in the neck area. Then using AE as the base, Le Brun constructs a second equilateral triangle with the vertex at D, and with ED parallel to BC. If the vertex D falls at some part of the animal's mouth, as with the lion, the animal is carnivorous; if not, as with the ox *(Plate 5)*, it is herbivorous or graminivorous (a grain-eater).

The loss most to be regretted in the missing dissertation is the comparison of man with the monkey. Two centuries before Darwin, Le Brun was examining the facial similarities between the two with scientific intent. He could not help but have been aware that in eyes, ears, and even mouth the monkey was closer to man than it was to any of the other animals he pictured; what conclusions he drew from that, if any, we will never know. But they were probably not very revolutionary. He was a religious man, conscientious in religious observances. And it was the seventeenth century. In that age of religious literalism, didacticism, and intolerance, it is unlikely that Le Brun would have allowed an inkling of Darwin's eventual heresy to lodge in his mind.

After the final experimentation of sketching first the ox with half a dozen different kinds of eyes and then the lion and the horse with human eyes, Le Brun went on to the extensive series of lithographic renderings which comprise most of this book. Whatever lack of merit these drawings have for us in a scientific sense, their ingenuity and draftsmanship cannot be denied. It's true that Le Brun stretched verisimilitude a bit in his eagerness to make the humans match the beasts, but if poets are allowed license, why not painters? The drawings are quite obviously the work of a man who in himself combined unusual powers of observa-

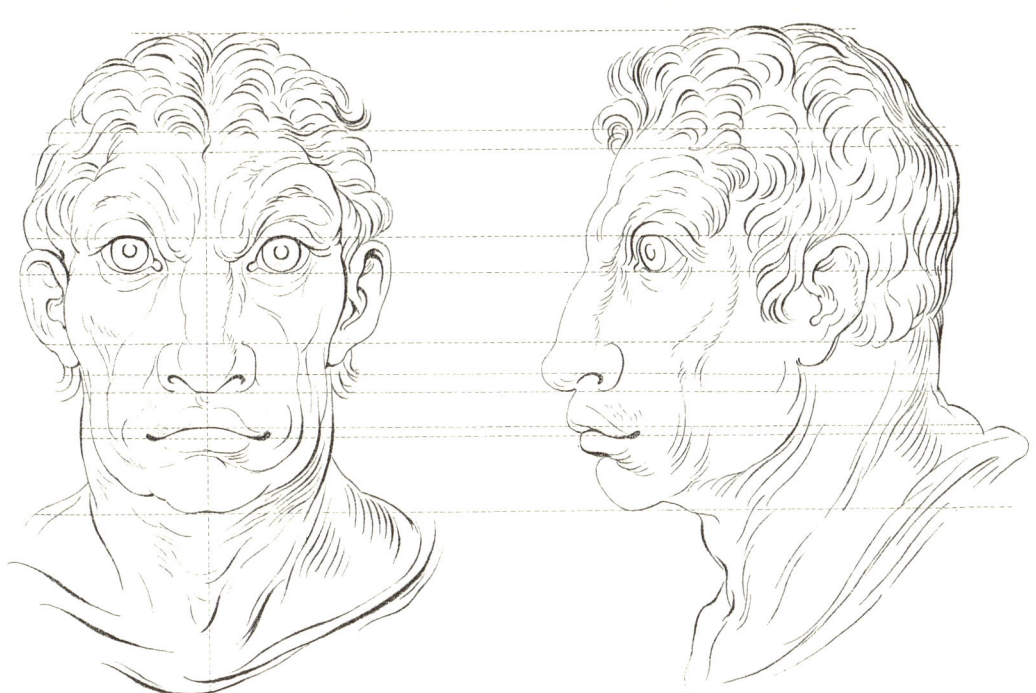

tion with a clever pen and brush and, I suspect, a real sense of humor. And the subject of the physiognomy studies is one of enduring interest. We continue to search for a sure way to predict character from countenance. We want to be able to trust and love with confidence; to know that the person with kind eyes will be a gentle friend, that the man with a chin of rocklike integrity will not abscond with the savings we entrust to him.

On the other hand, there was the admonition of Le Brun's friend, La Fontaine, in his fables: "Beware, as long as you live, of judging people by appearances."

Edward Sorel

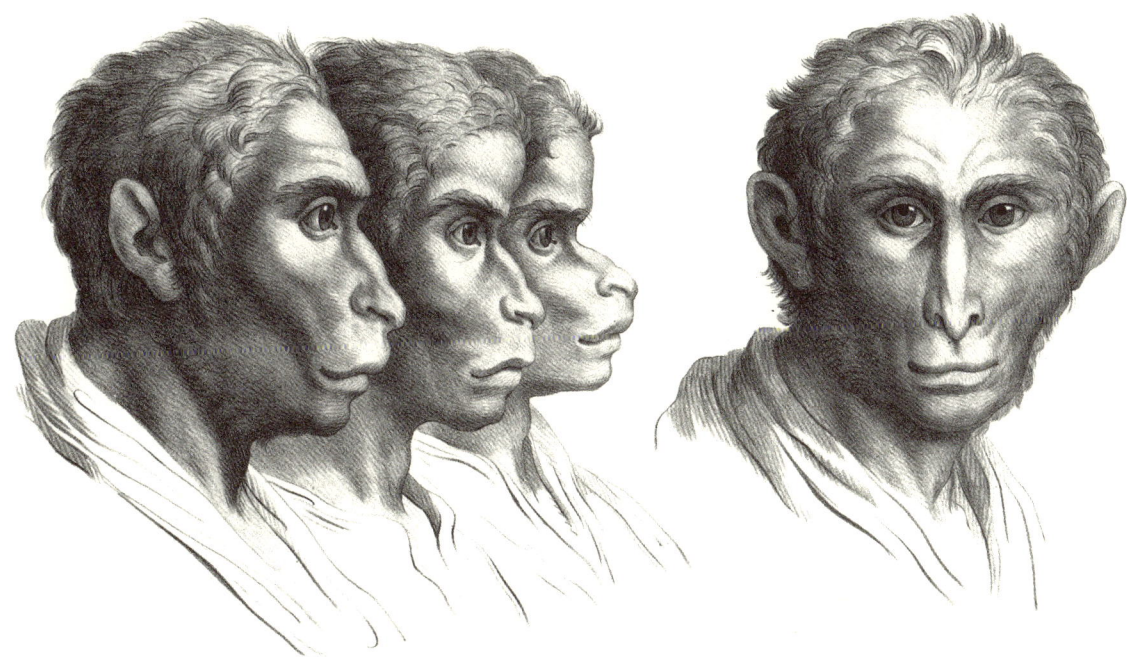

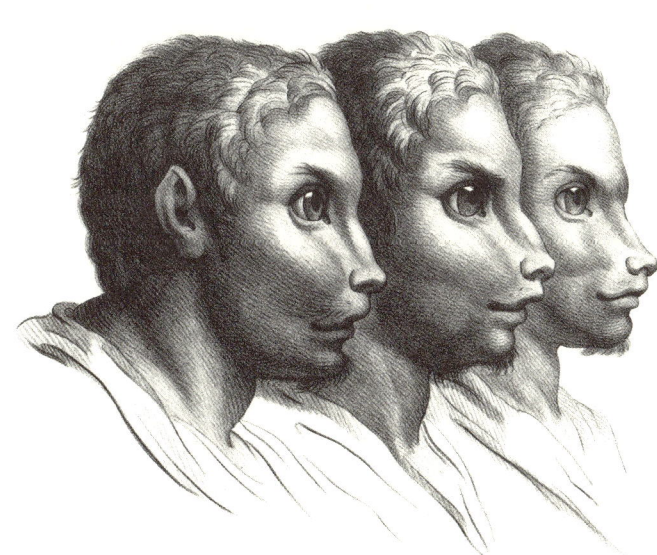

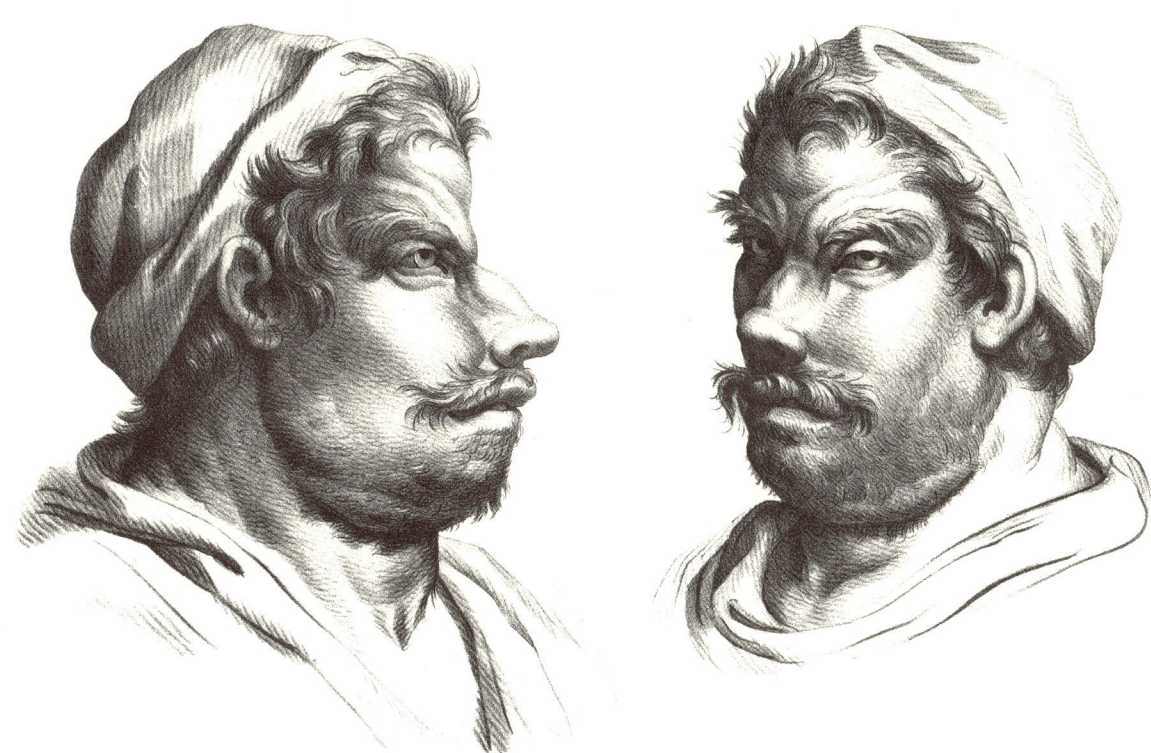

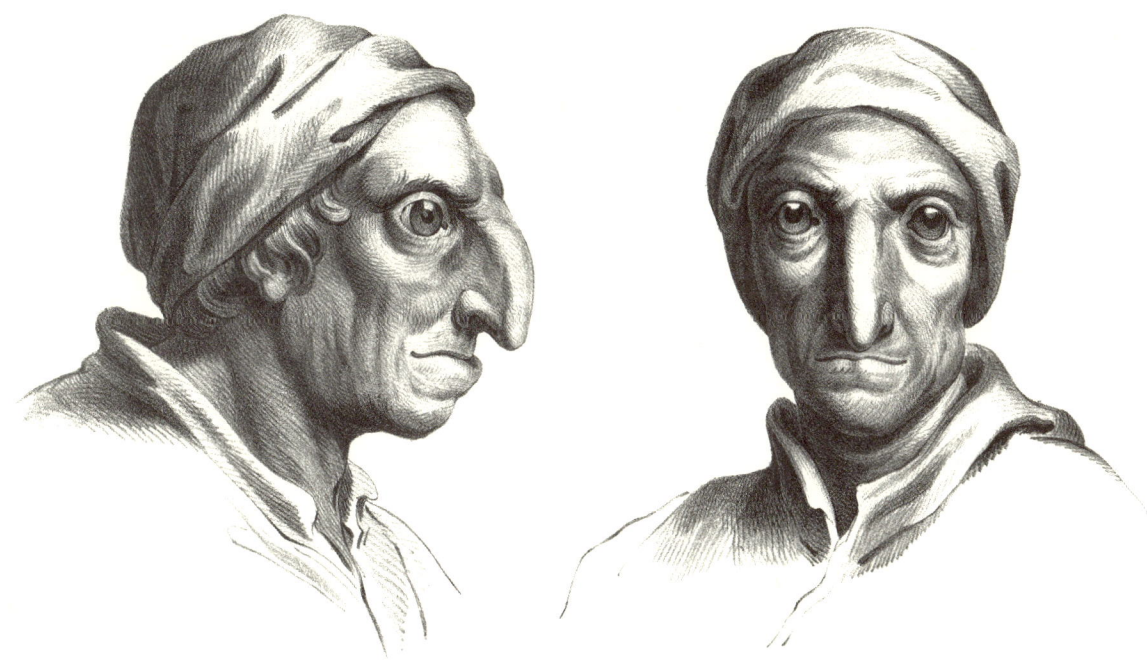

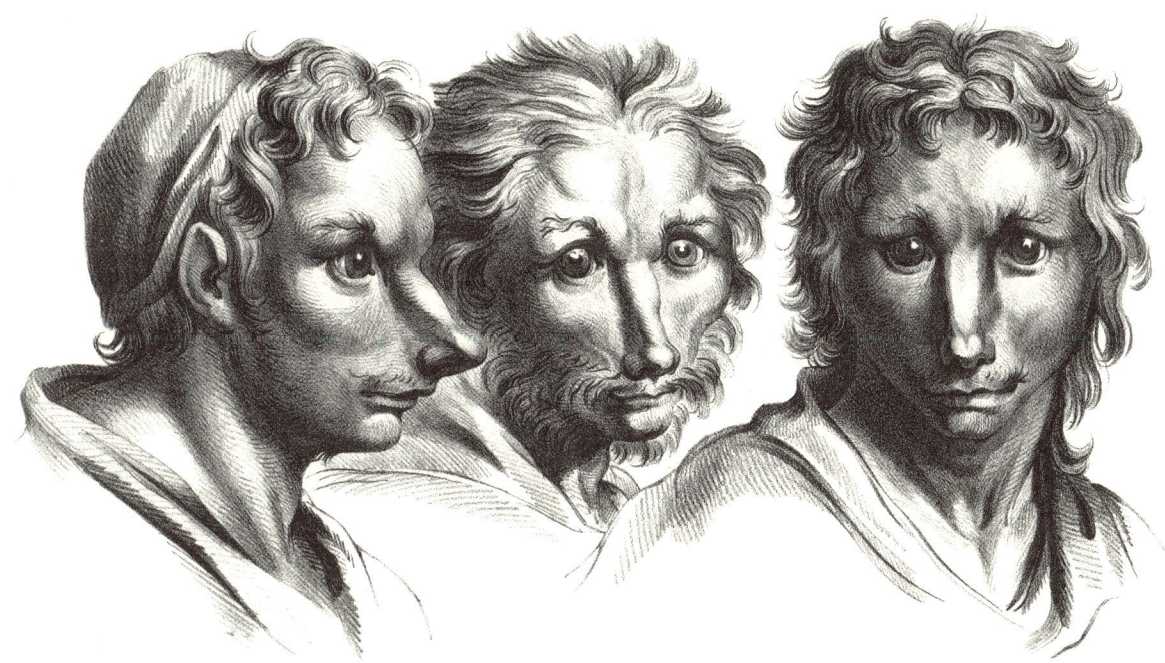

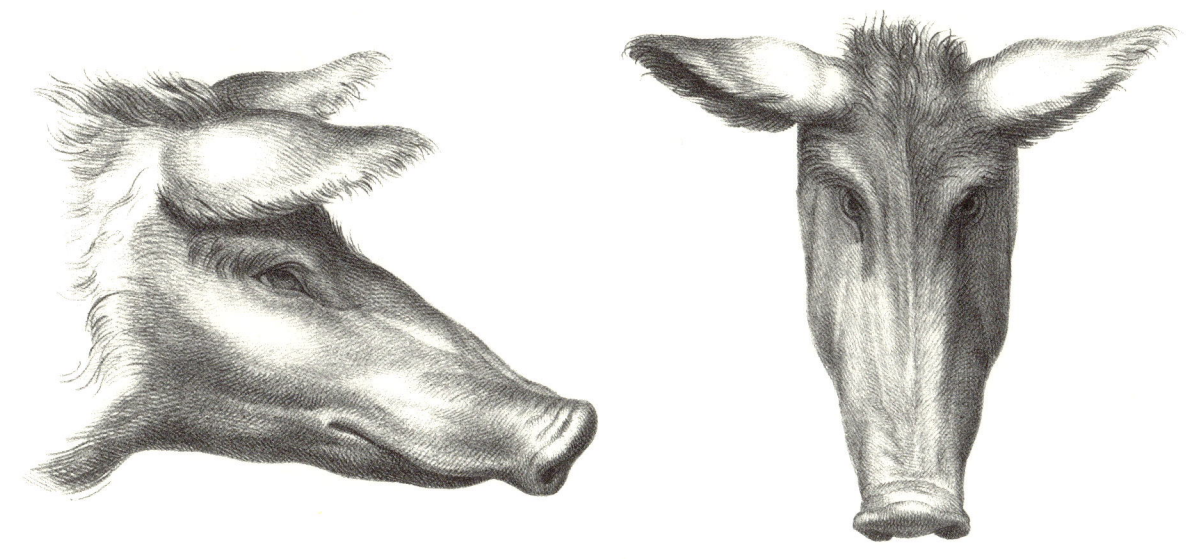
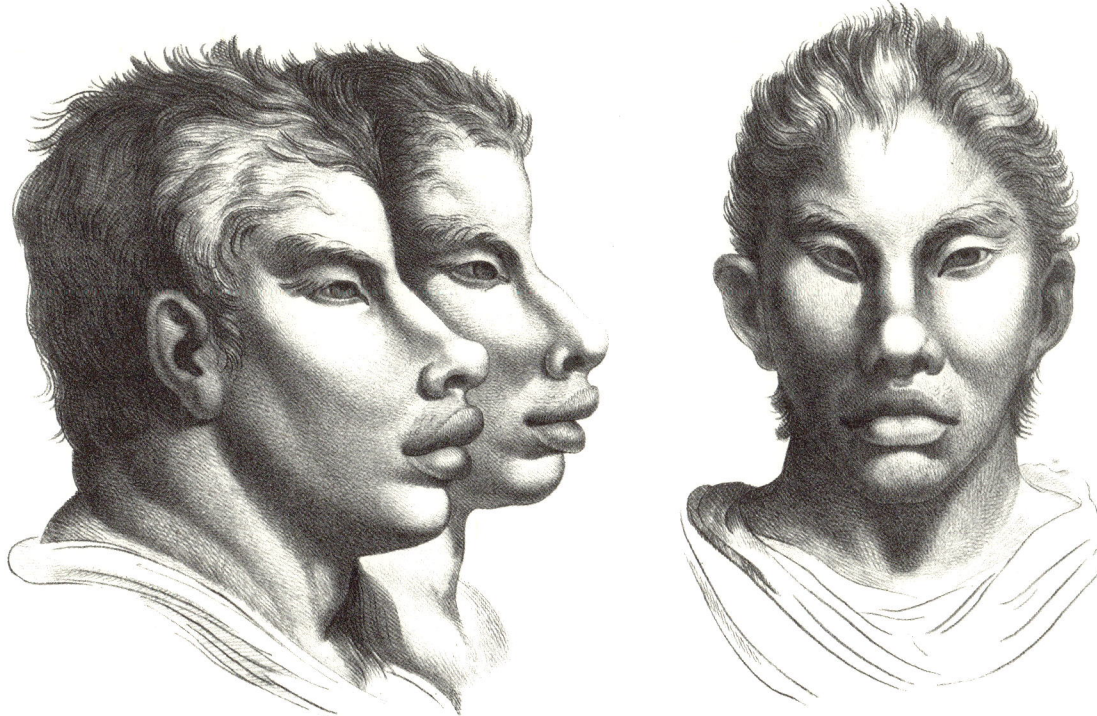

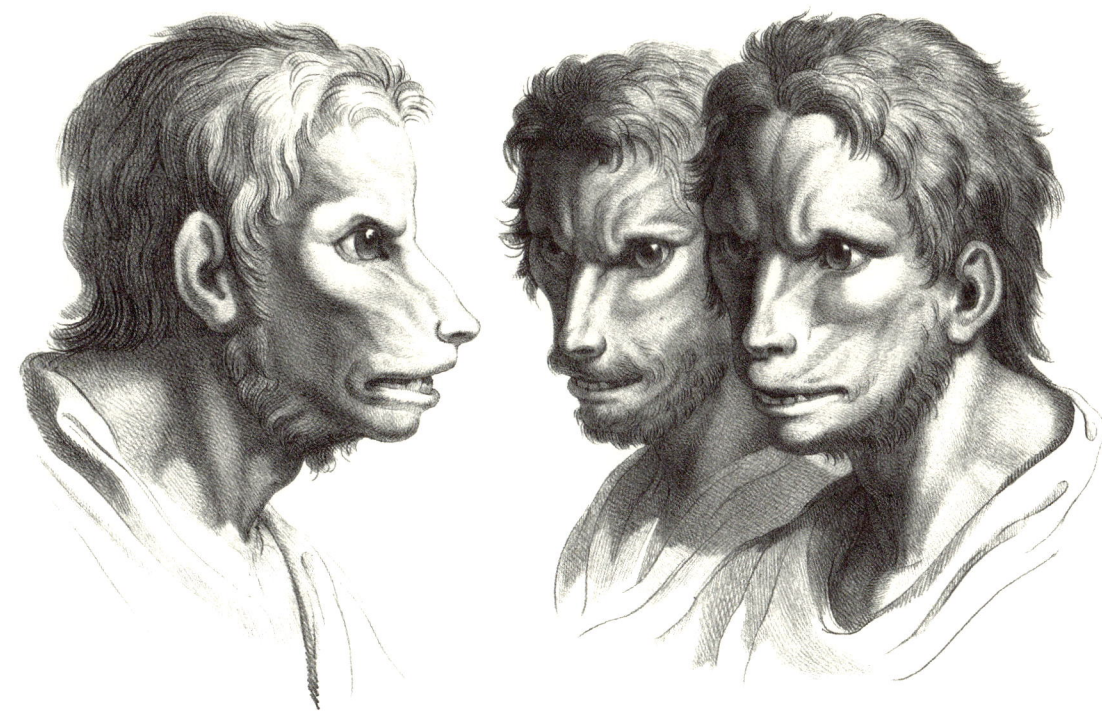

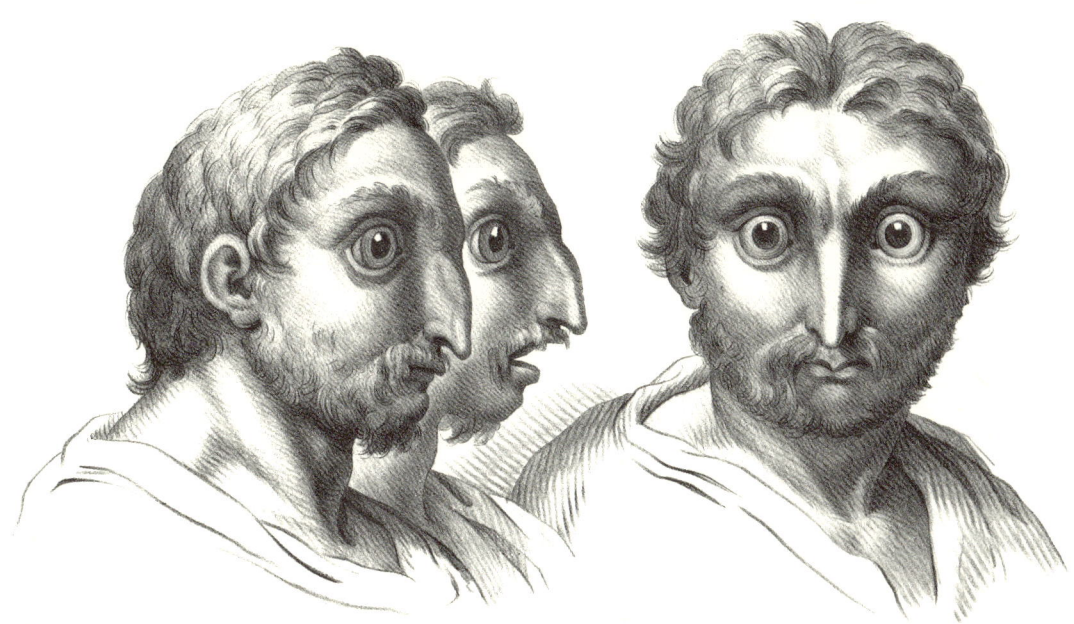

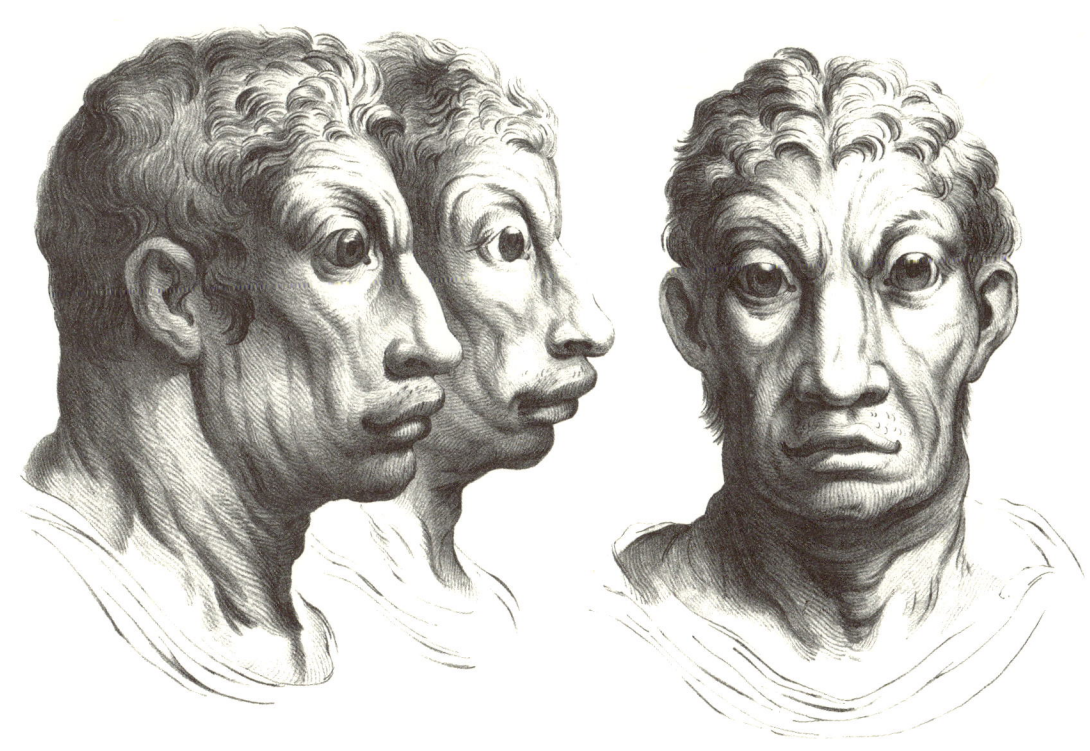

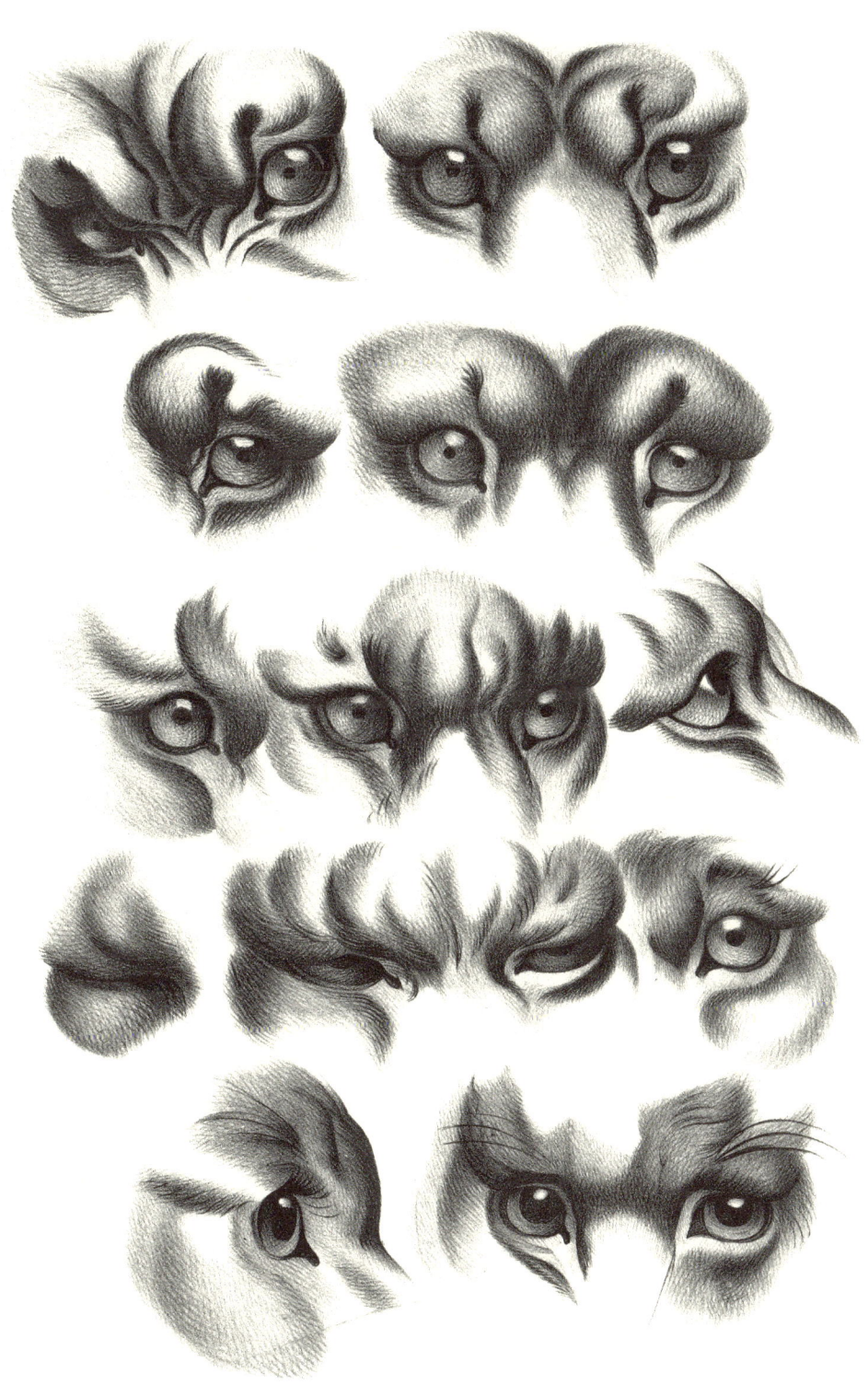

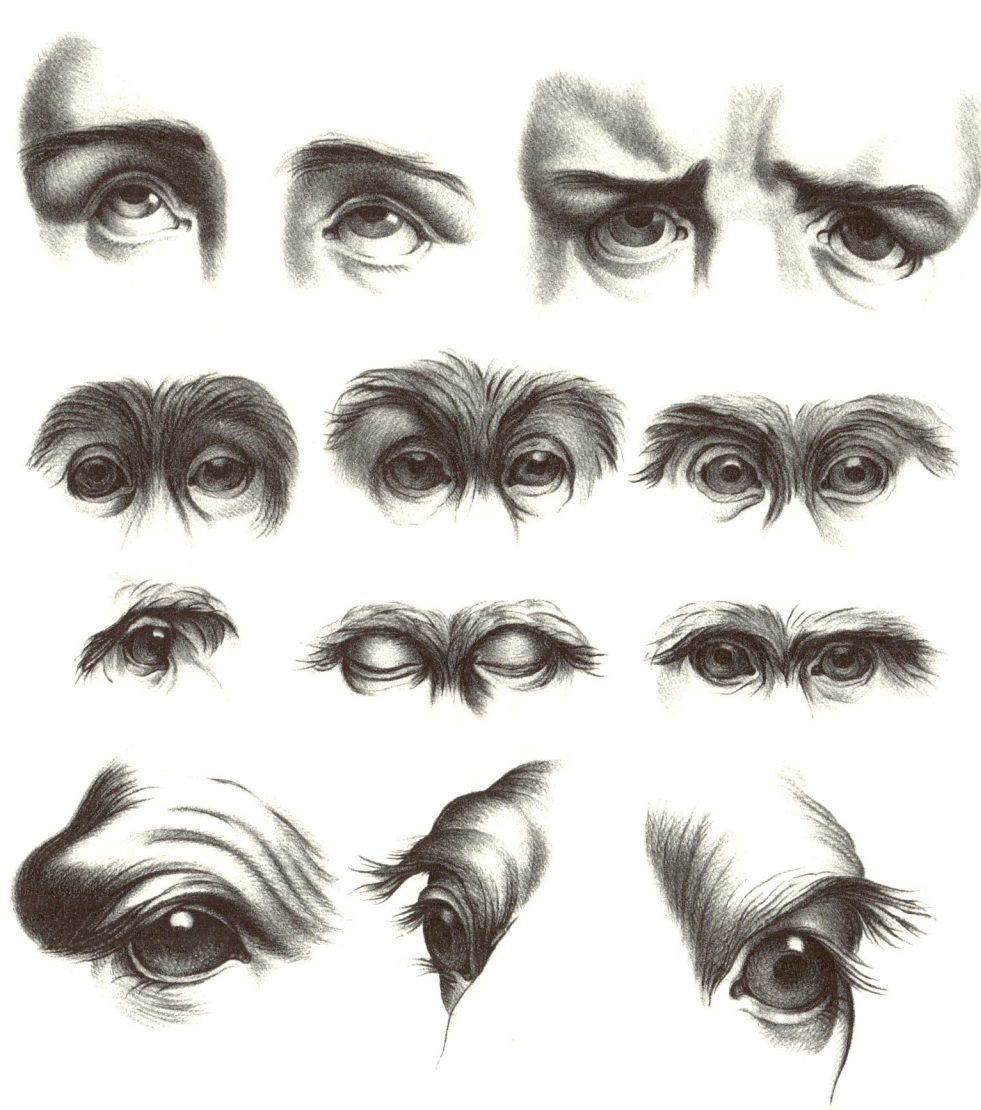

The text of this book
was set by Johnson/Kenro, Inc.,
Freeport, New York,
in Bodoni Roman.
The text stock
is 100# Soft White
Superfine Text
supplied by
The Baldwin Paper Company,
New York City.
The book was printed
by Halliday Lithograph,
West Hanover, Massachusetts.
and bound
by A. Horowitz and Sons,
Fairfield, New Jersey.
Patrick Couratin
designed the book.